Happy Barrel Raku Kiln

How to build your own barrel raku kiln

By Jesse Rasmussen

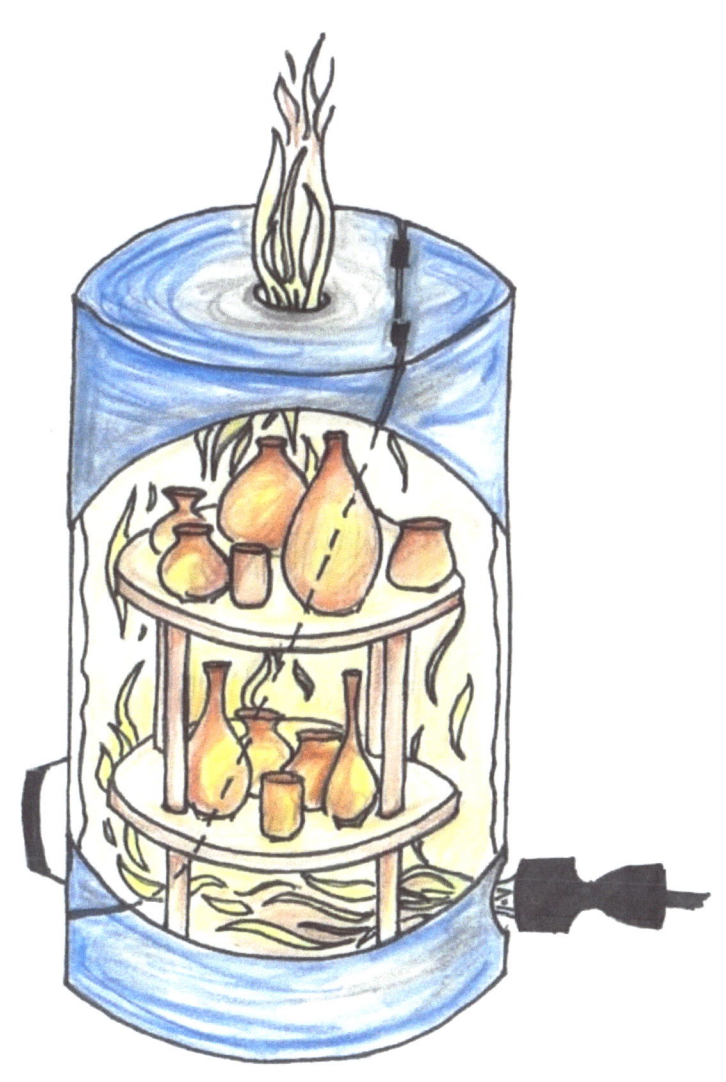

Happy Barrel Raku Kiln:
How to build your own barrel raku kiln

By Jesse Rasmussen

MFA University of Sydney, Sydney College of the Arts
BFA Minnesota State University, Mankato

Editorial and publishing: Paula Schumacher / UpMesa Publishing

Cover illustration: Madeline Klusmire

Copyright © 2017 Jesse Rasmussen
All rights reserved.

Artist's website: jesserasmussen.blogspot.com
Instagram: @jesseceramics

ISBN-13: 978-1976278327
ISBN-10: 1976278325

- Introduction 4
- Precautions 4
- Tools 5
- Materials 5
- Make Buttons 6
- Mark Areas To Be Cut 7
  - BURNER PORT HOLE 7
  - CHIMNEY 8
  - DOOR OPENING 9
- Cutting and Attaching Parts 11
  - CUT OUT BURNER PORT AND CHIMNEY 11
  - CUT BOTTOM OF DOOR 12
  - CUT TOP OF DOOR AND WELD HINGES 13
  - WELD HANDLE ON DOOR 14
  - CUT SIDES OF DOOR 15
  - CLEAN UP 15
  - DRILLING HOLES FOR BUTTONS 16
  - LINING THE KILN WITH FIBER 18
- Shelves, Bricks, and Burner 22
- Congratulations—you've built a Happy Barrel Raku Kiln! 25
- Burners 25
- Maintenance and Care 26
- Firing tips 26
- About the Author 27

Introduction

This book will give you step by step instructions on how to build your own barrel raku kiln that is easy to use, efficient and portable. The kiln design can also be used to bisque fire pots as well as fire to cone 6 when used with a proper burner.

Please enjoy and have fun with the design, modifying it as you see to fit for your specific needs.

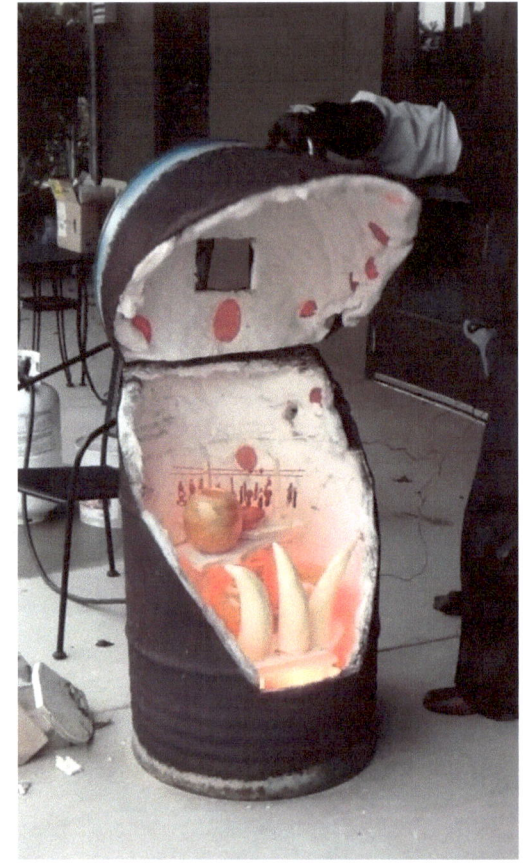

Precautions

As with any building project, your safety is a top priority. Wear appropriate safety equipment when constructing this kiln.

Recommended Safety equipment:

- Mask or Respirator. P100 or N95 masks should be used when cutting or installing Cerawool.

- Rubber gloves. Rubber gloves should be used when handling Cerawool.

- Welding equipment. Welding is required for this project and proper welding safety equipment should be used.

This book is intended to guide you through the steps to build your own raku kiln. It does not provide any information on how to fire your kiln. <u>Knowledge and experience on firing and operating kilns is required to complete this project.</u> Standard safety precautions when firing the kiln should be taken.

Tools
You will need the following items to build your kiln:

- Wire cutters
- Pliers
- Welder
- Grinder with metal cutting and grinding disc
- Sharp scissors
- Box cutter
- Rope or string
- Marker
- Ruler or tape measure
- Drill
- 1/16" Drill bit

Materials
The following is a list of materials you will need to complete your kiln.

- An empty metal 55 gallon oil drum. (Oil drums that formerly stored nonflammable materials are recommended.) Cutting into barrels with flammable material is dangerous and should be done by a professional.
- Clay – A strong stoneware clay body is recommended.
- 18 Gauge Nichrome Wire.
- 2' x 18' x 1" thick Cerawool rated for 2300° F or higher (Cerablanket, or Superwool are common names for this fiber).
- 2-3 sturdy stainless steel metal hinges.
- 1 stainless steel handle (large enough to use comfortably with gloved hands).
- 1" x 15" x 1/8" thick steel (optional).
- 6 Hard bricks (soft bricks can be used but tend to be fragile).
- 1 Kiln shelf (size should be no bigger than 19" and shape can vary depending on what is available in your area).
- Additional kiln shelves and posts are optional.
- Small scrap kiln shelf for damper.
- 20 pound propane tank.
- Gas regulator.
- Gas hose.
- Burner (covered more in the burner section).

Make Buttons

Using your clay, cut out round circles from a slab. These will be used as buttons to hold the fiber in place on the kiln.

The clay should be about ¼" thick and around 3" in diameter. You will need 35 buttons, and back up buttons are a good idea as they will need replacing as time goes by.

Drill or poke 2 holes in the buttons. Your hole size will depend on your specific clay shrinkage rate, but a hole around 3/16" should be fine.

Bisque fire the buttons, and then fire to the recommended temperature for strength and vitrification of the clay body.

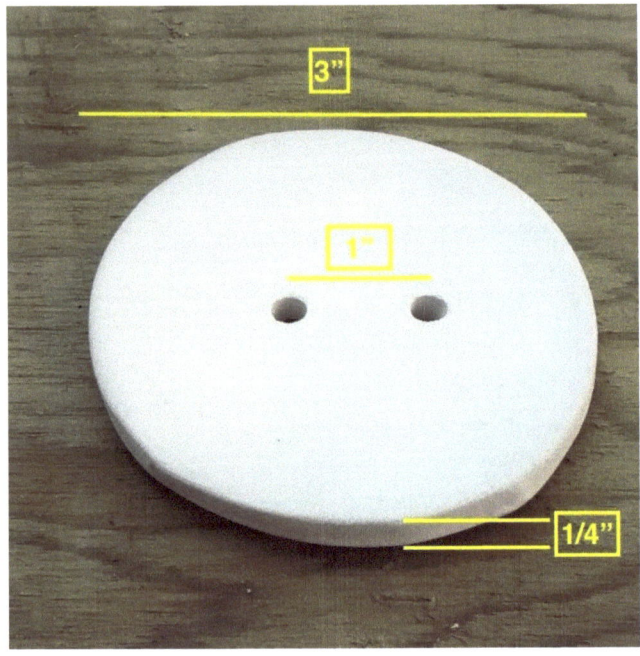

Figure 1: Clay button

Mark Areas To Be Cut

You will need to mark all areas on the barrel to be cut. Determine where the front and back of the kiln will be. (Hint: it's round so it doesn't really matter.) A guide line in pencil or marker can be drawn down the middle of the barrel and through the center of the top to help keep things straight.

BURNER PORT HOLE

On the back of the kiln, measure up from the bottom 2 ½" and mark a square that is 5 ½" wide and 4 ½" tall. This will be your burner port, and it should be around 1" larger than your burner to allow for proper airflow.

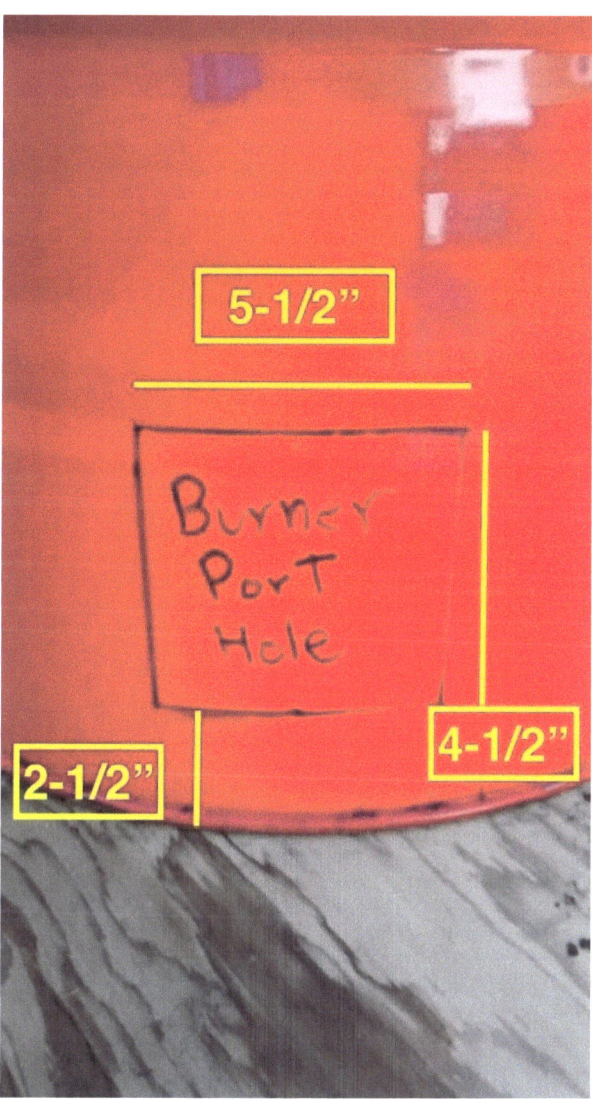

Figure 2: Markings for Burner Port Hole

CHIMNEY

On the top of the kiln, find the center and mark with an X.

Directly above the burner port, measure in 5" towards your middle mark. Using a straight edge, draw a line from point A to your center mark.

Using a square, draw a perpendicular line to both edges (point B and Point C). This will be your hinge line.

Draw a rectangle in the top, middle of your kiln 5 ¾" long and 4 ½" wide. This will be your chimney.

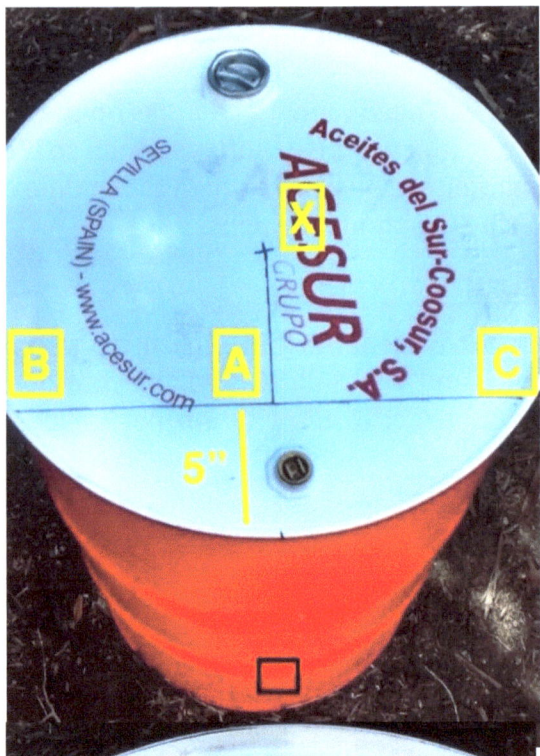

Figure 3: Markings to locate chimney

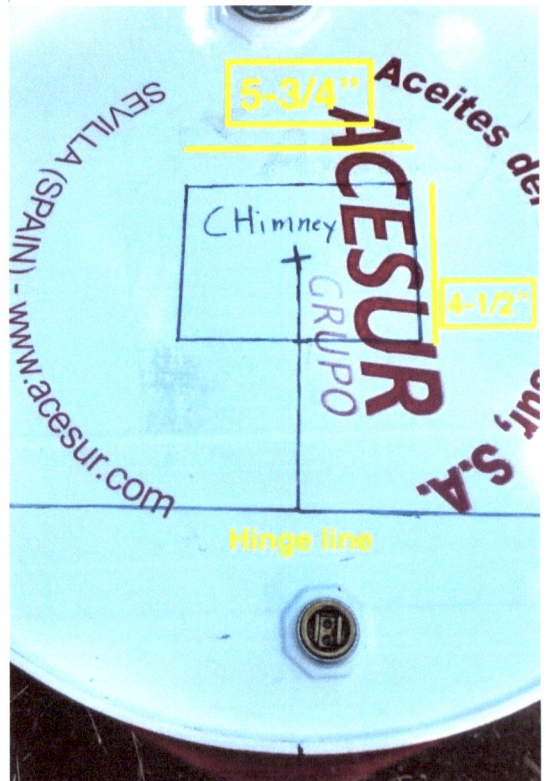

Figure 4: Markings for chimney

DOOR OPENING

Mark the point directly opposite of the burner port on the top side, and draw a dotted guide line down the front of the kiln. (Remember: Do not cut the dotted line!)

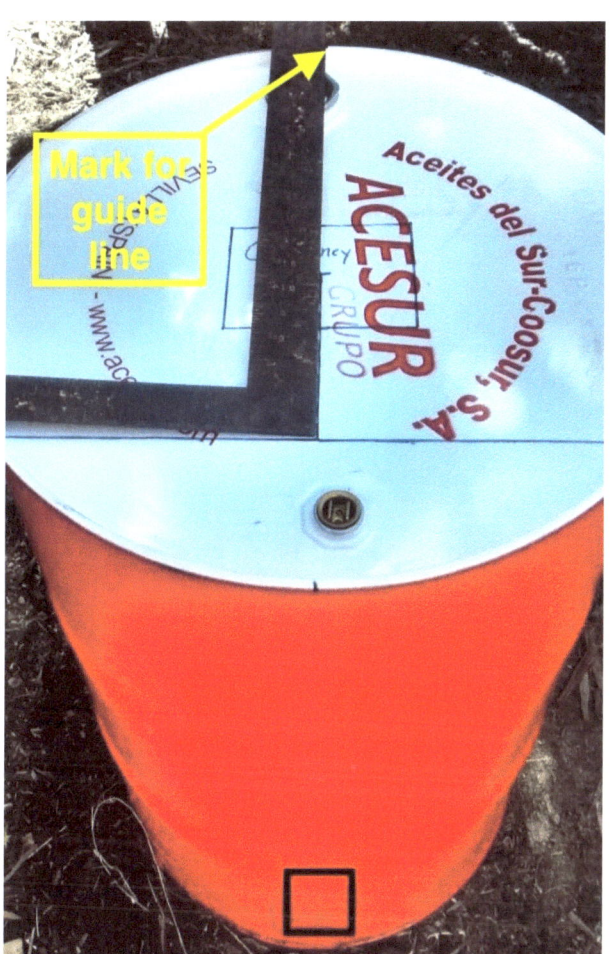 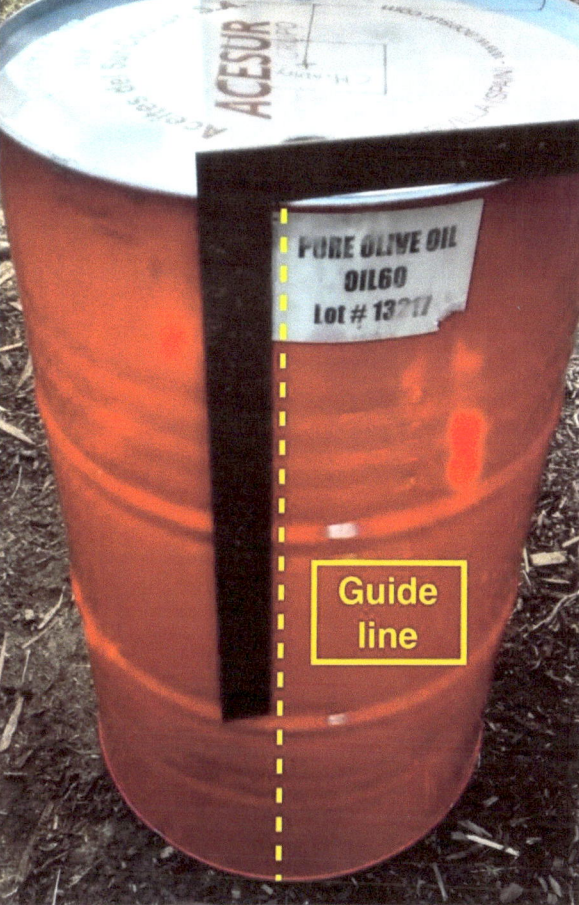

Figure 5: Markings to locate the door opening

From the bottom center point, measure over on both sides 5 1/8" then measure up 10" on each side and mark points D and E.

Connect points D and E. This is the bottom of your door.

For the sides of the door, draw a line connecting points C and D on the one side and connecting points B and E on the other side. (Hint: a string line and tape is helpful.)

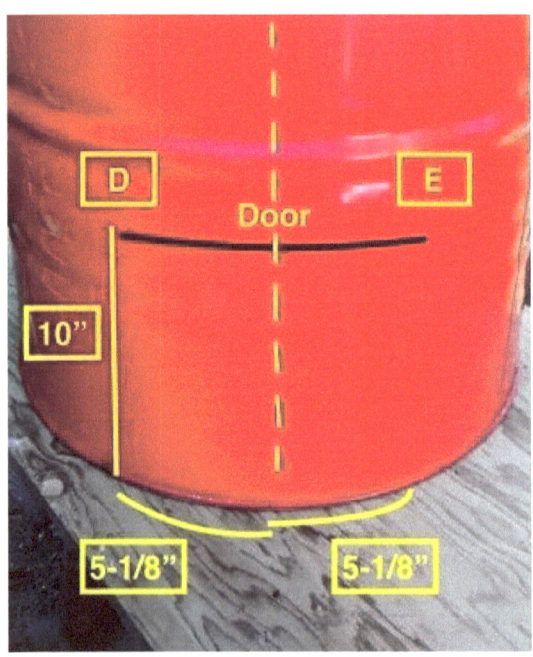
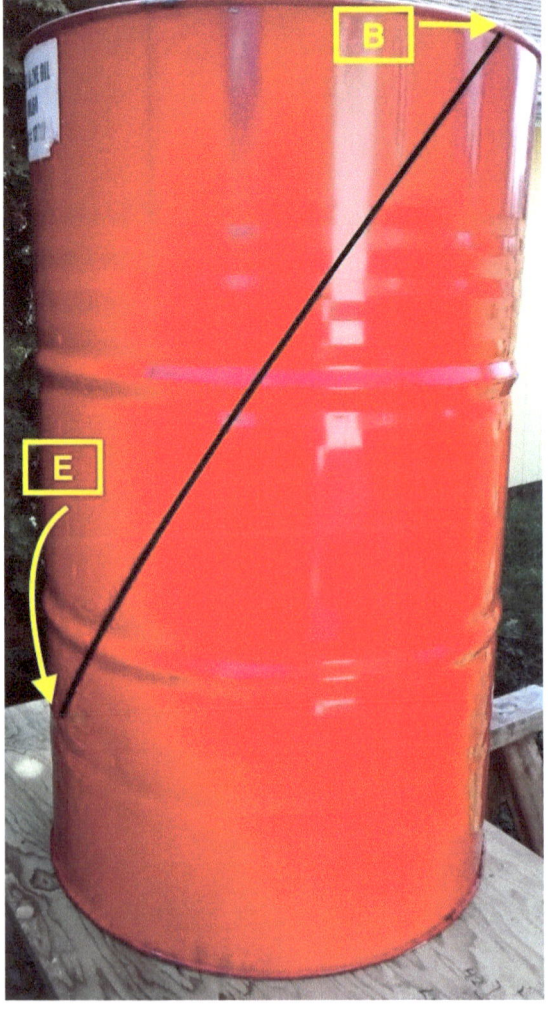

Cutting and Attaching Parts

This guide shows attaching parts to the kiln using a welder. An alternative to using a welder is by drilling holes and attaching with appropriate sized stainless steel nuts, washers, and bolts. When using bolts, the complete door will need to be cut before attaching hardware.

CUT OUT BURNER PORT AND CHIMNEY

Use an angle grinder to cut the square burner port and chimney.

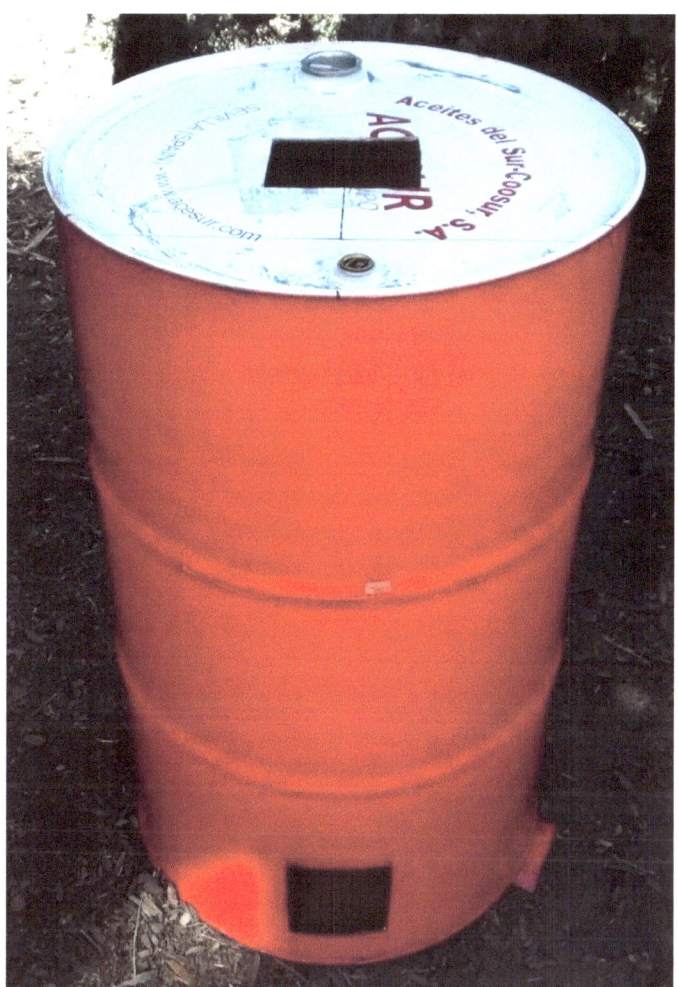

Figure 6: Cut out burner port and chimney

CUT BOTTOM OF DOOR

Cut the bottom of door with an angle grinder from Point D to Point E.

For easier handling of the kiln during construction, transportation, and storage, use two angle brackets and wing nuts to hold the bottom of the door to the body of the kiln. They are optional, but very handy.

Weld the angle brackets into place 1" from Point D and Point E.

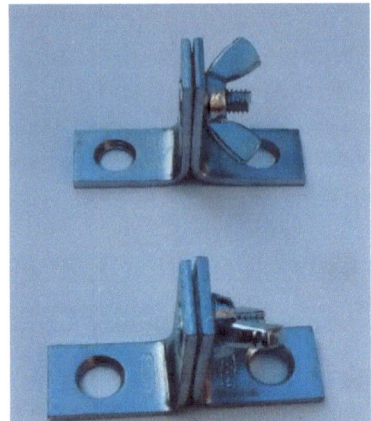

Figure 7: Optional angle brackets and wing nuts

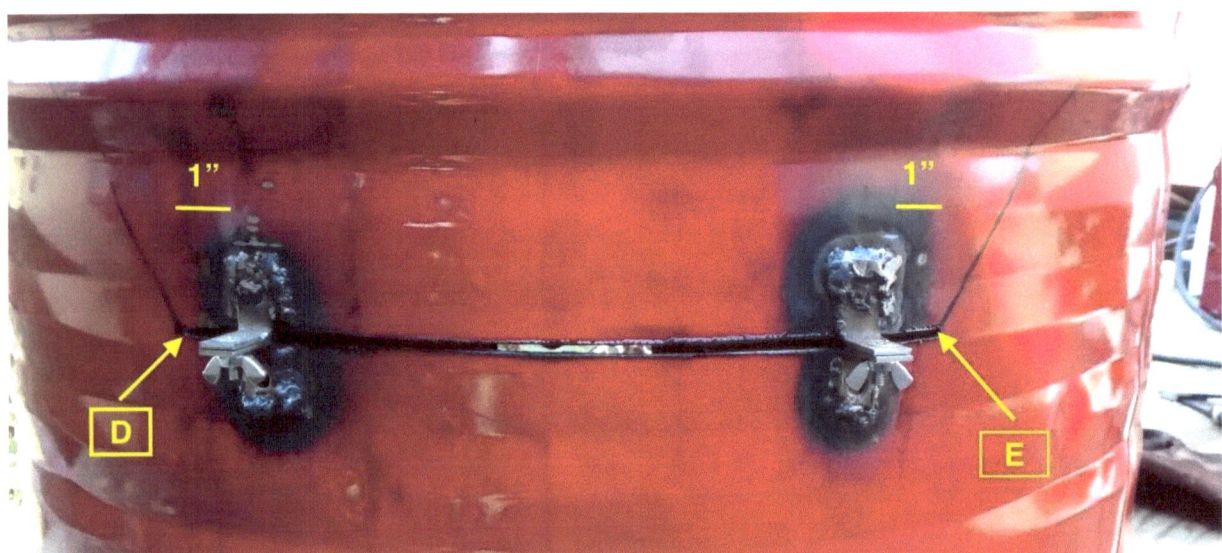

Figure 8: Angle brackets and wing nuts welded to bottom of door for better handling of kiln

CUT TOP OF DOOR AND WELD HINGES

Cut the top of the door (Point B to Point C). This is also called the hinge line. Weld 2 hinges. Position the first one 3" in from Point B. Position the second one 3" in from Point C.

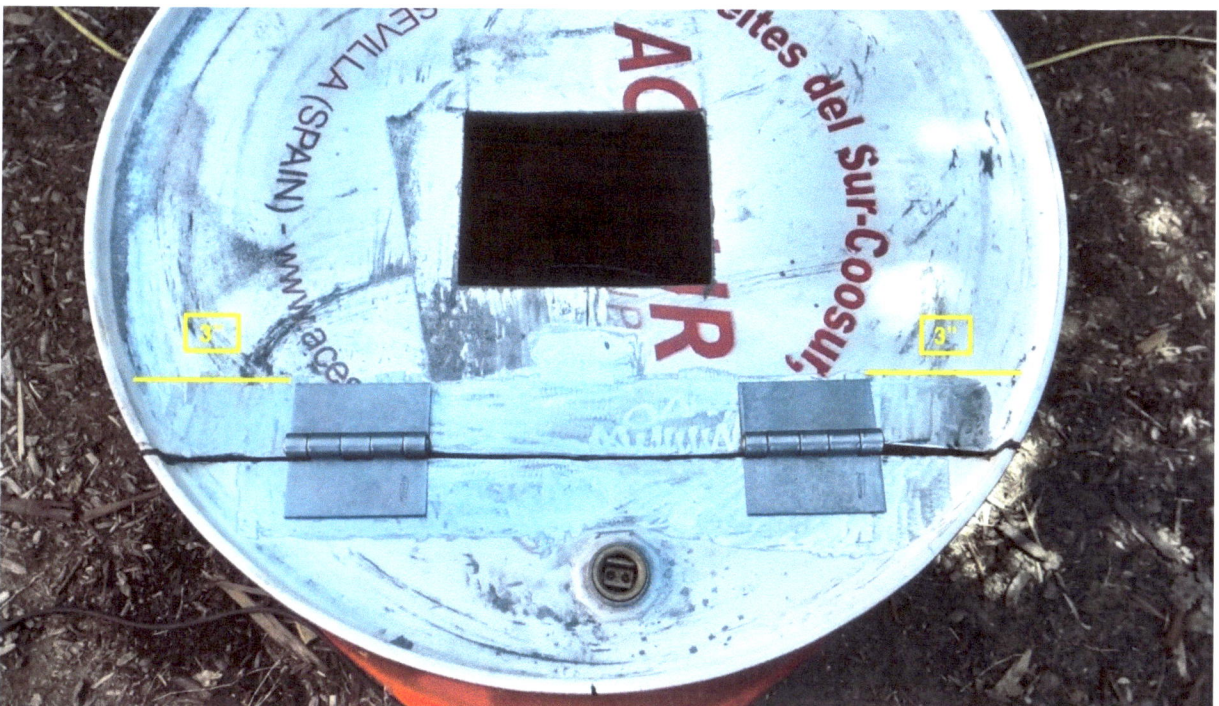
Figure 9: Placement of hinges on the top of door

Optional: Weld a flat bar across the hinge line to provide support. This will help counteract metal warping over long periods of frequent use. To do this: use 1" by 1/8" thick metal, cut 2 strips 15" long and weld along hinge line. Then weld hinges into position.

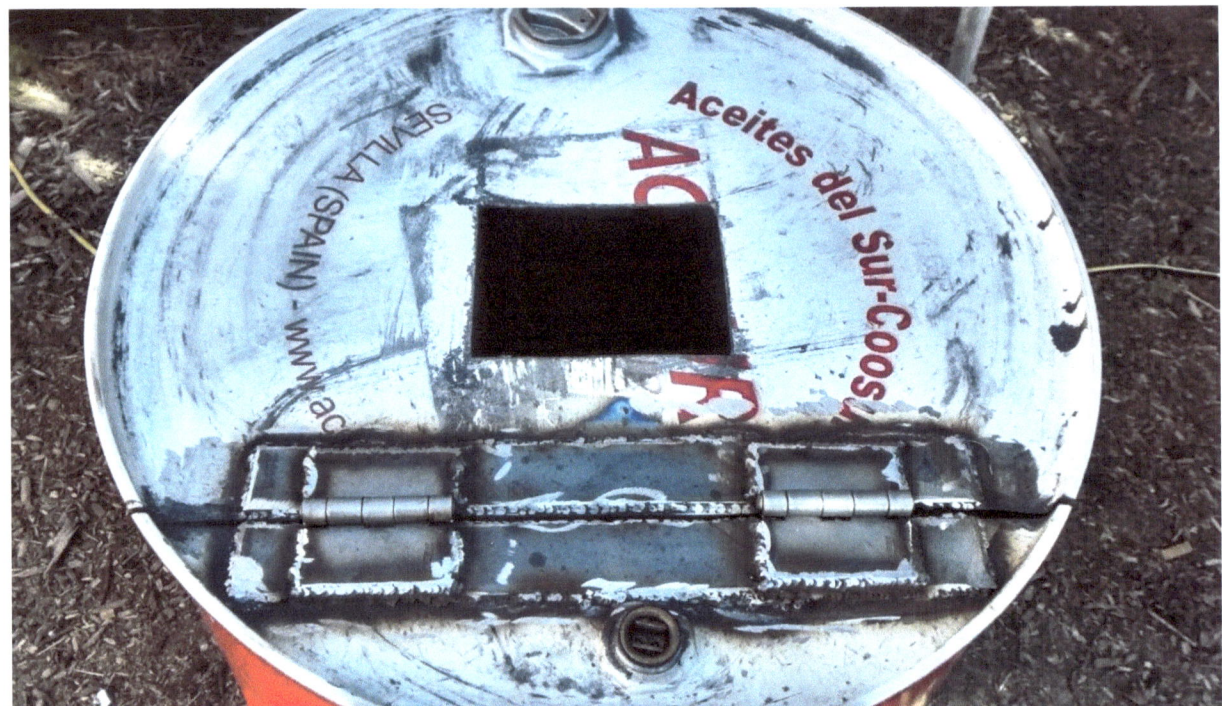
Figure 10: Hinges with flat bar (for added strength) welded to top of door

WELD HANDLE ON DOOR

Weld the handle 16" from bottom of the door, centered.

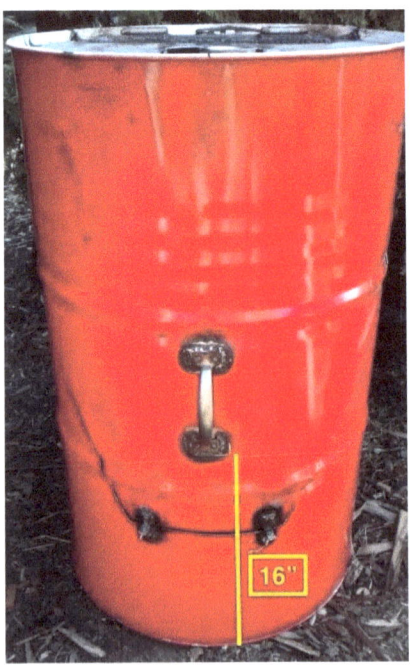
Figure 11: Handle welded to door

CUT SIDES OF DOOR

Cut the remaining areas of door. Cut Point C to Point D, and then cut Point B to Point E.

Unscrew the wing nuts at the bottom of the door; remove the machine screws, and open door.

CLEAN UP

Grind or file edges and clean out any residue inside of the barrel. (Most metal burs will burn off in the first firing.)

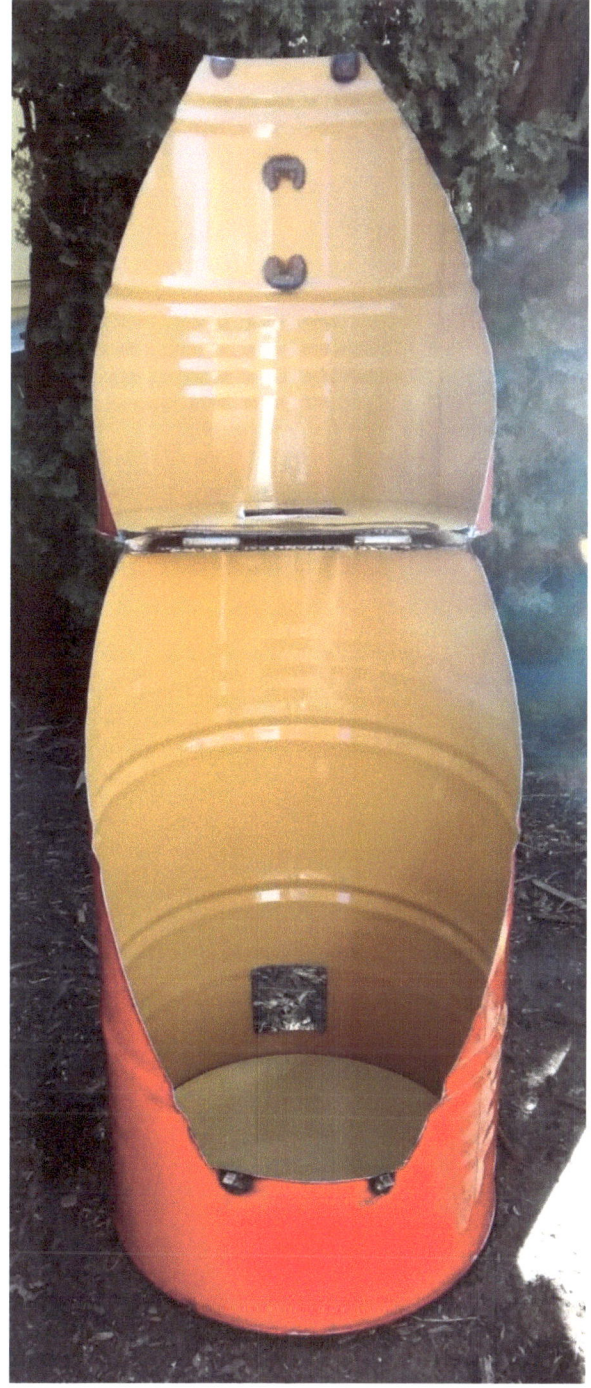

Figure 12: All cuts made and hinges installed

DRILLING HOLES FOR BUTTONS

Drill holes into the barrel for securing the buttons to the inside of the kiln. For each button, drill 2 holes, 1" inch apart.

Exact placement of the buttons is not necessary. The important thing to remember is that the buttons are 3" wide so holes should be 2-3" from edges and openings.

Buttons will need to be placed in areas where the fiber has a seam or is close to an opening such as around the door, burner hole, and chimney.

Since the fiber is 24" wide, your first button holes should be 21" up from the bottom of the kiln. Then at 26" from the bottom of the kiln for the next layer of fiber, followed by buttons 3" down from the top of the kiln.

Button placement should be around 10" inches apart (side to side) to hold in the fiber. Additional buttons can be added later if the fiber slumps.

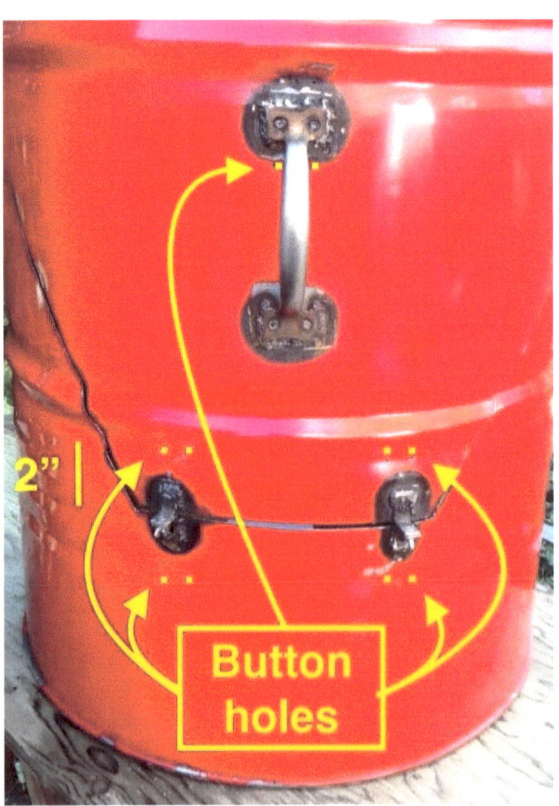
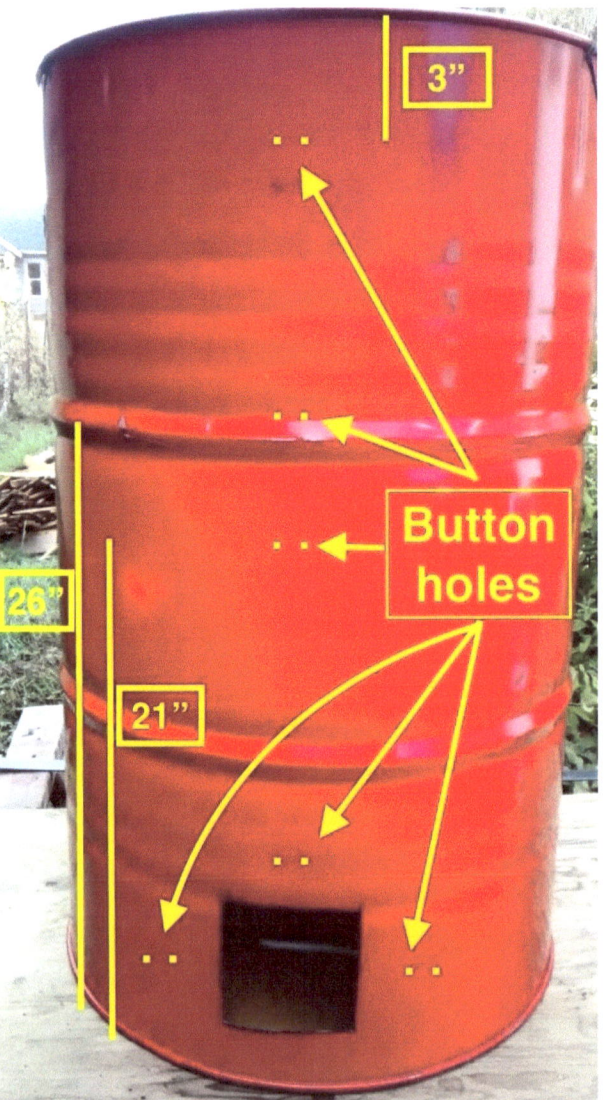

Figure 13: Button hole placement

Add button holes to the top of the kiln around hinge line and chimney (it is helpful to lay out the buttons and mark where they will go on the inside of the kiln). The bottom of the kiln will not need any buttons.

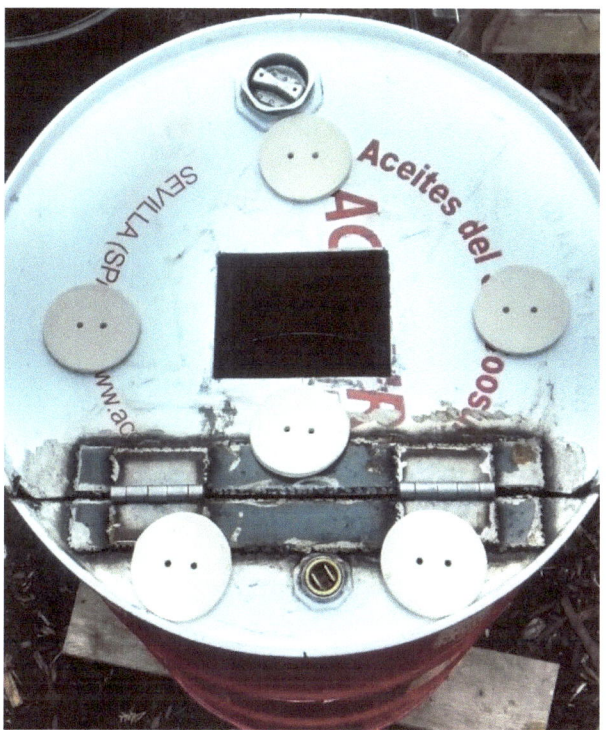
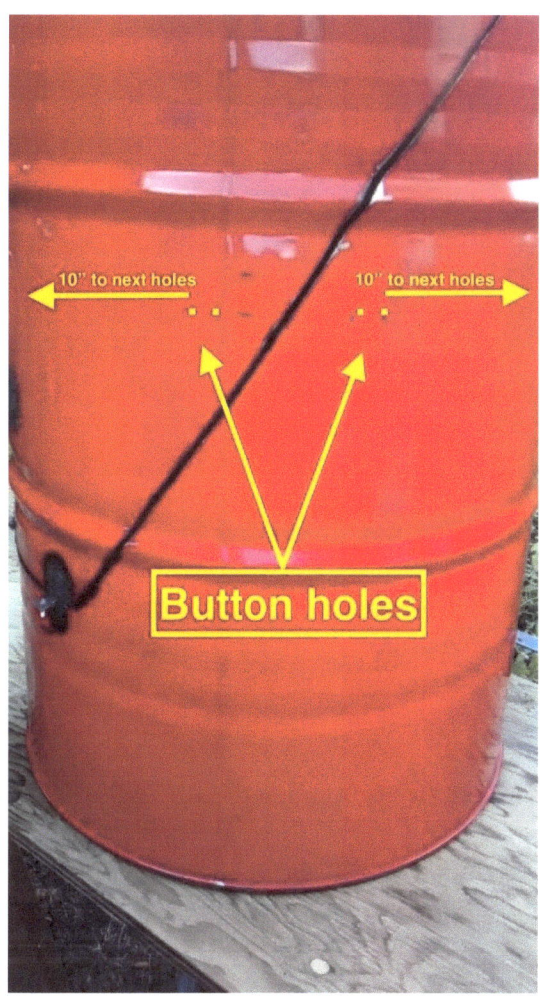

LINING THE KILN WITH FIBER

You need to wear a P100 or N95 mask, gloves, and safety glasses when cutting or handling the Cerawool.

Measure the diameter of the kiln and cut the Cerawool to that length using a box cutter.

Using the barrel as a guide, draw a circle and cut the Cerawool. You need two circles: one for the bottom and one for the top of the kiln.

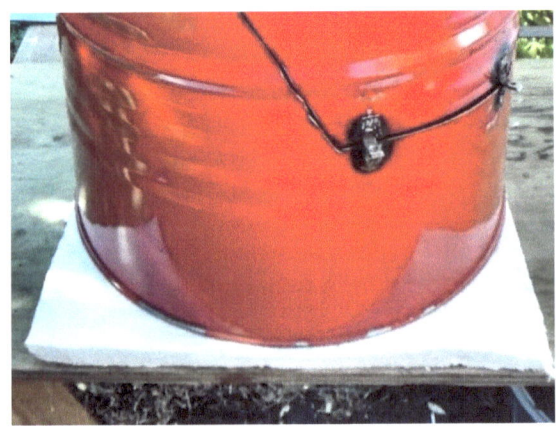

Figure 14: User barrel to mark circle pattern

Insert one of the circular shaped fibers into the bottom of the kiln. It should be a snug fit.

Cut Nichrome wire into lengths approximately 8" long and bent into a "U" shape. You will need these for every button (around 35).

It is easiest to poke the Nichrome wire in from the outside of the barrel, through the predrilled holes, through the Cerawool, and through the button holes. Then hold the wire tight and twist to secure the button on the inside.

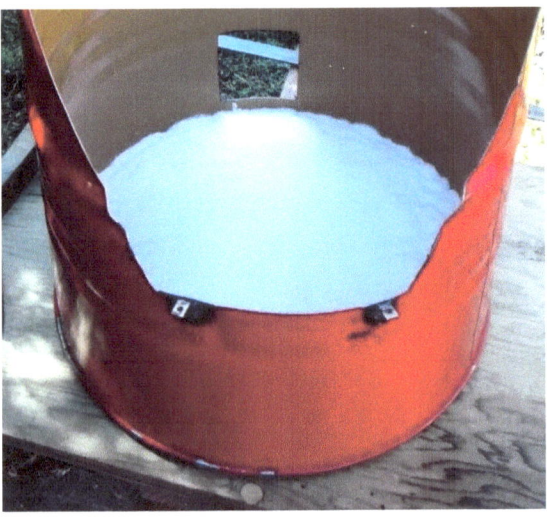

Figure 15: Cerawool fits snugly in bottom of kiln

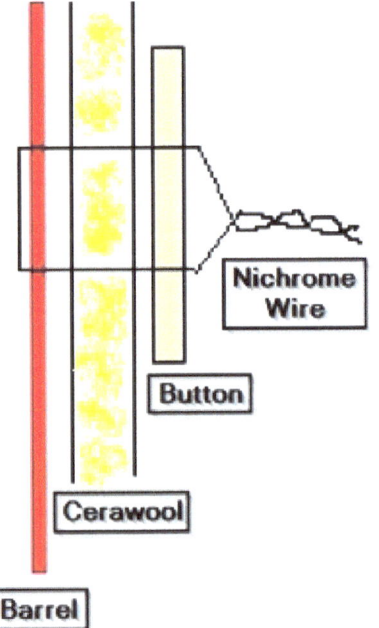

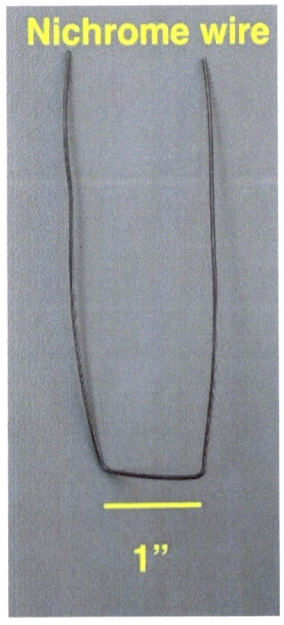

Install the second circular shaped fiber on the top of the kiln, and cut along the hinge line. Then attach the fiber that was just cut to the remaining top section. This part can be tricky as the door needs to be partially open, so having a friend help or propping the door with a wooden block helps.

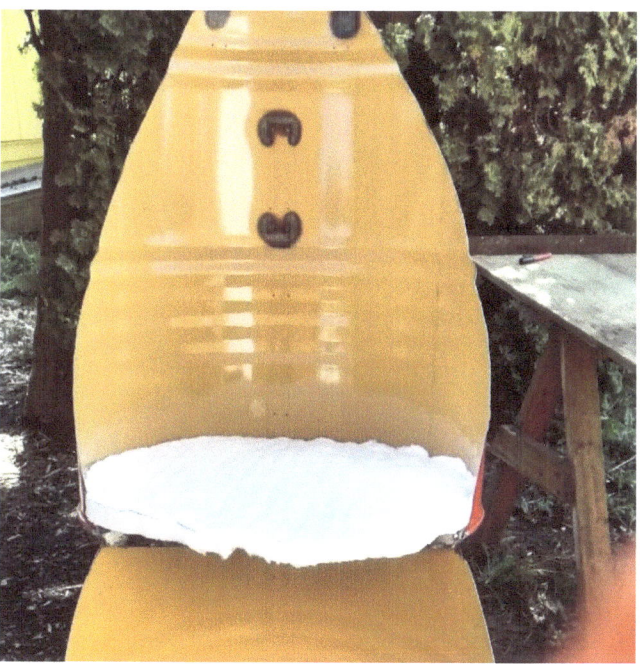
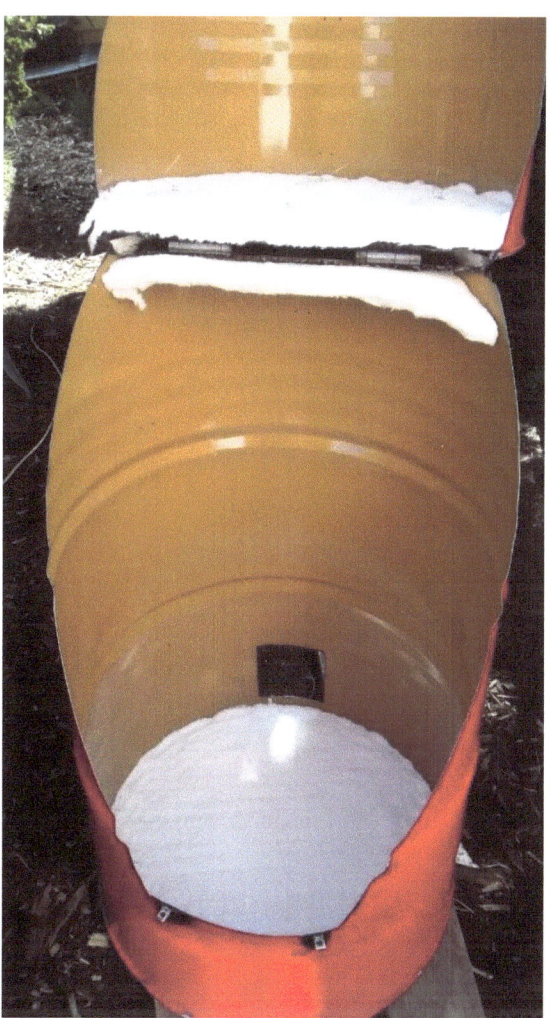

Figure 16: Cerawool fit for the top of the kiln

Using a rope, Measure the circumference of the barrel and cut the Cerawool to that length (cut it a little longer than needed just to be sure). Start installing fiber on the bottom of the kiln, attaching with buttons as you go.

Cut the excess Cerawool off where door is. It can be helpful to leave ¼" overhang around the door for a snug fit.

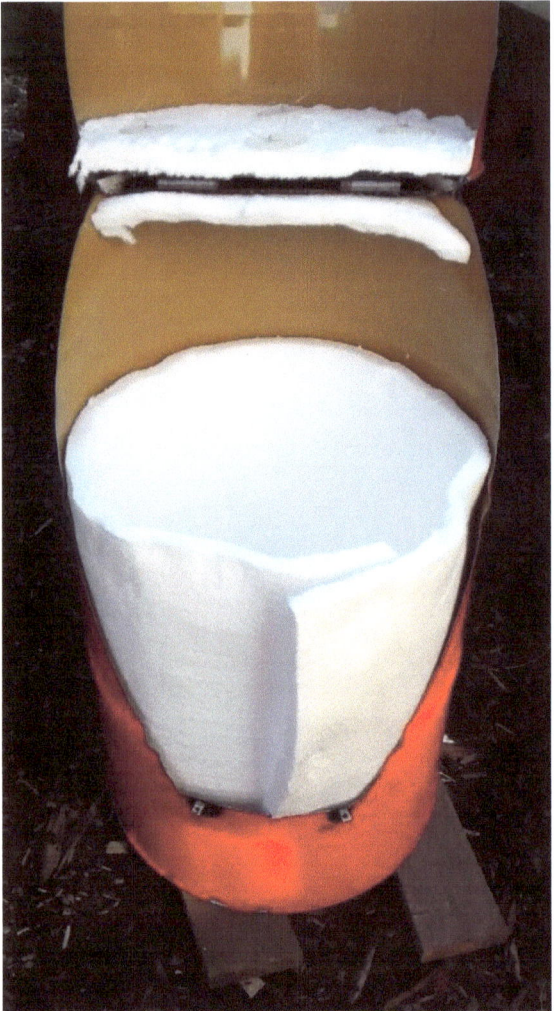 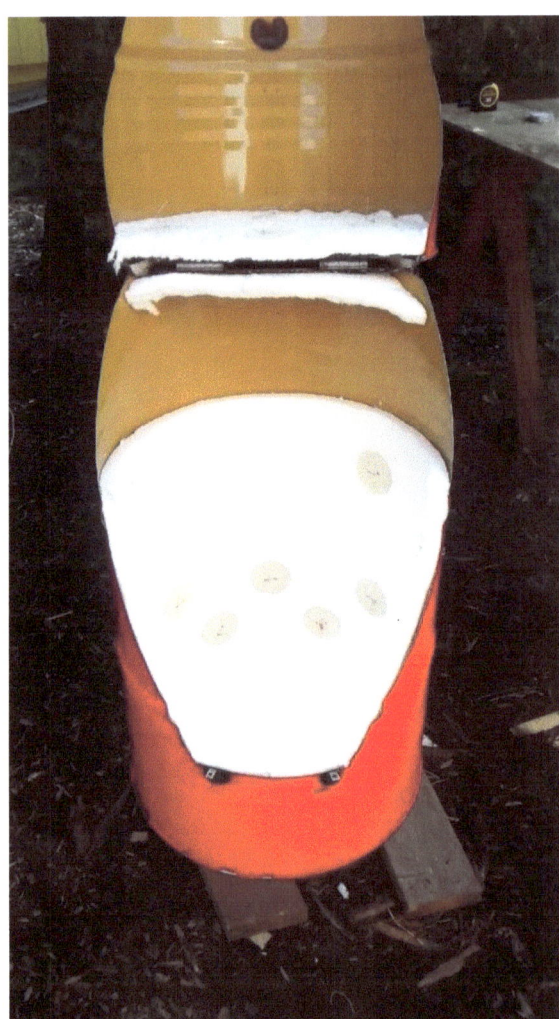

Figure 17: Cerawool fit for the body of the kiln

Continue to add Cerawool, secure it with buttons, and cut off the extra fiber around the door opening. With the fiber is completely installed, cutout the openings for the chimney and the burner port. Trim all extra wire, and trim any loose fiber with a scissors.

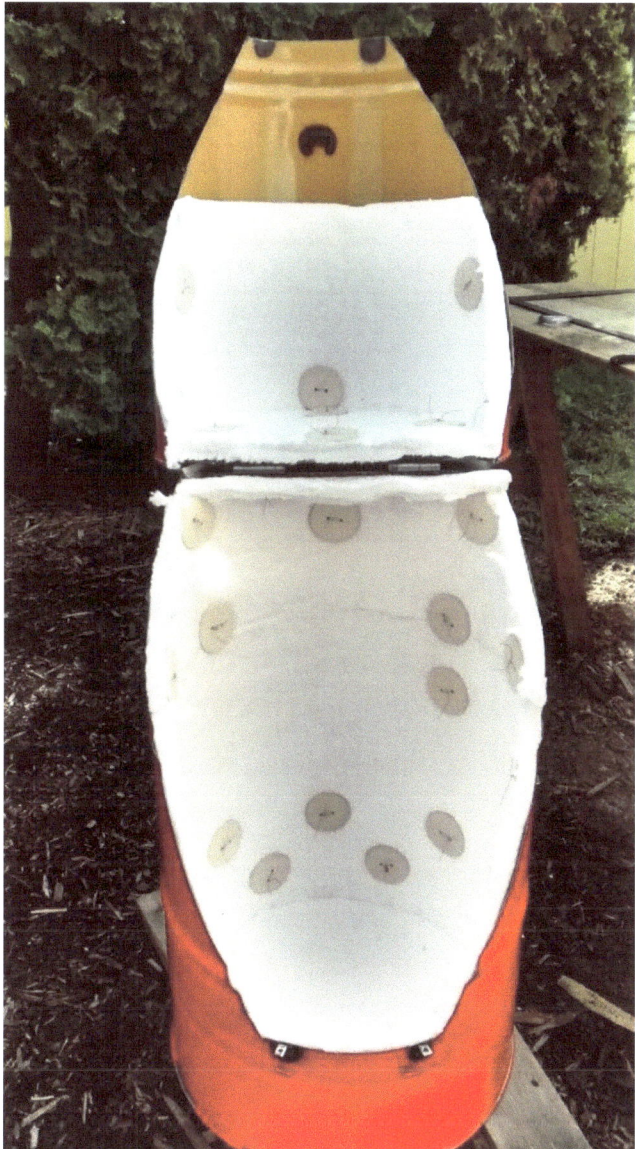
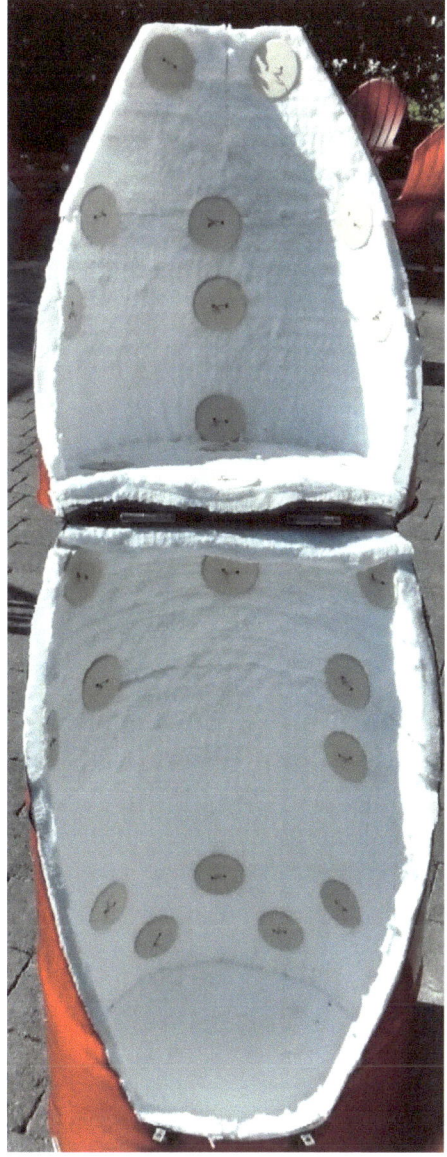

Figure 18: Fiber attached to inside of kiln with buttons

Shelves, Bricks, and Burner

Place fire bricks in a triangle in bottom of kiln, leaving the burner port hole unblocked. Bricks should be around 3" from the side to allow for good air exchange.

Once the bricks are in place, trace around the bottom of each one, remove the bricks, and cut out the Cerawool where you indicated the bricks will sit.

Place a second layer of three bricks on top of the first layer in an alternating triangular fashion.

Place a kiln shelf on top of the bricks. There should be a gap of at least 1" between the shelf and the fiber to allow air flow.

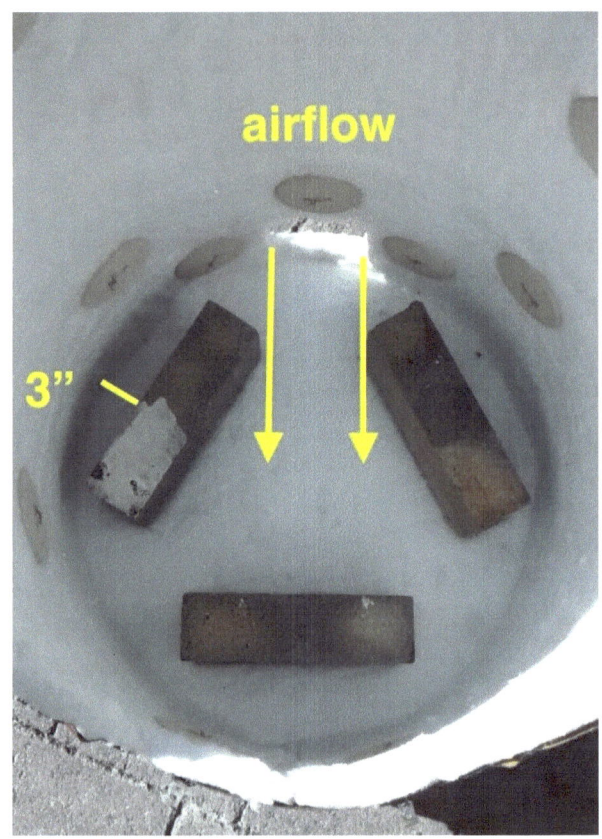

Figure 19: First layer of bricks

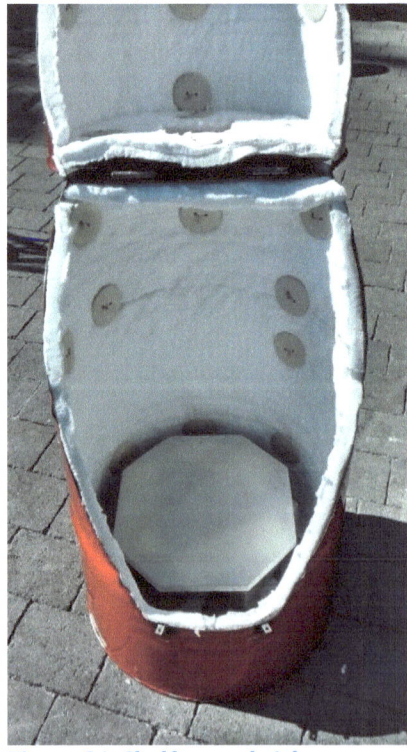

Figure 21: Shelf set on bricks

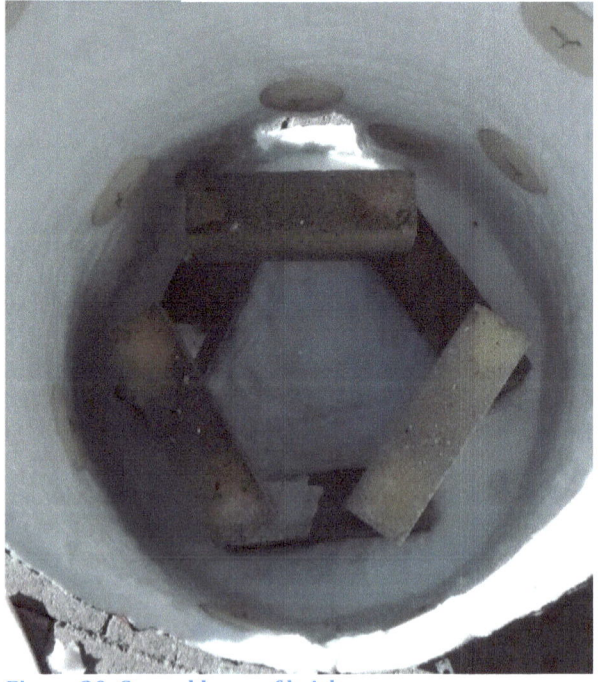

Figure 20: Second layer of bricks

On the outside of the kiln next to the burner port, place 2 bricks next to each other to hold the burner at the height of the burner port.

The burner should be placed with a ½" to 1" gap between the kiln and burner to allow for proper air intake. Kiln shards or additional bricks can be used to secure the burner in place.

Additional holes can be drilled for thermocouples if you plan on using a pyrometer. In this case, one was placed slightly above the bottom shelf and another is placed towards the top.

Additional shelves or half shelves can be placed on kiln posts to the desired height. When adding additional shelves, the firing temperature from top to bottom can be dramatically altered depending on the shelf size, size of work, and size of shelf. It is best to fire without additional shelves until you get to know your kiln.

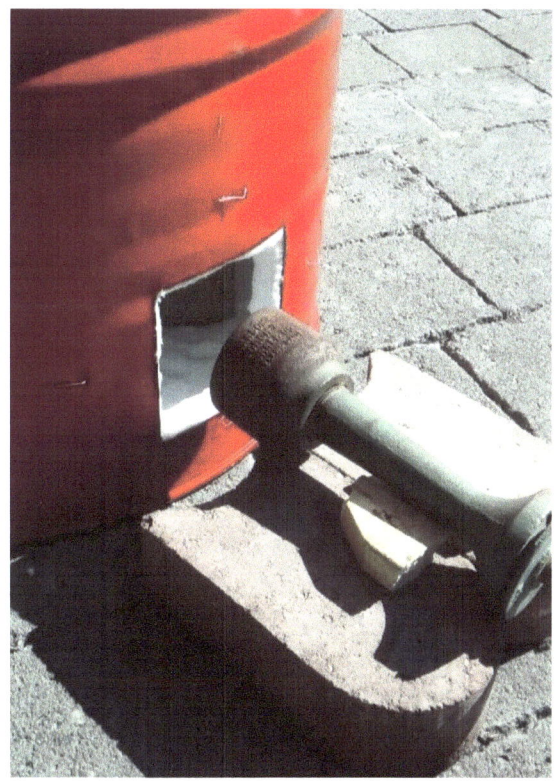
Figure 22: Burner placement

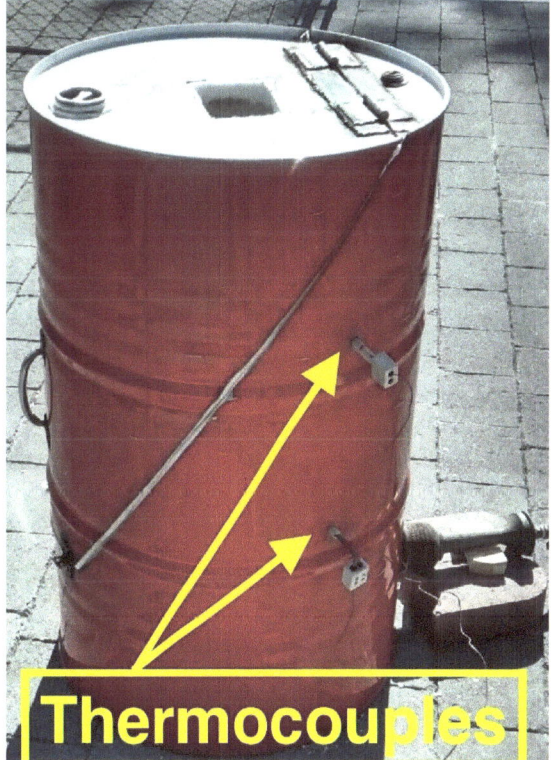
Figure 23: Thermocouples added

After loading kiln, place a kiln shard or left-over Fiber over the chimney to close off approximately 1/3 of the opening. This will be your damper and will regulate temperature and atmosphere when firing. It will have to be adjusted during the firing, and 1/3 closed is a good place to start.

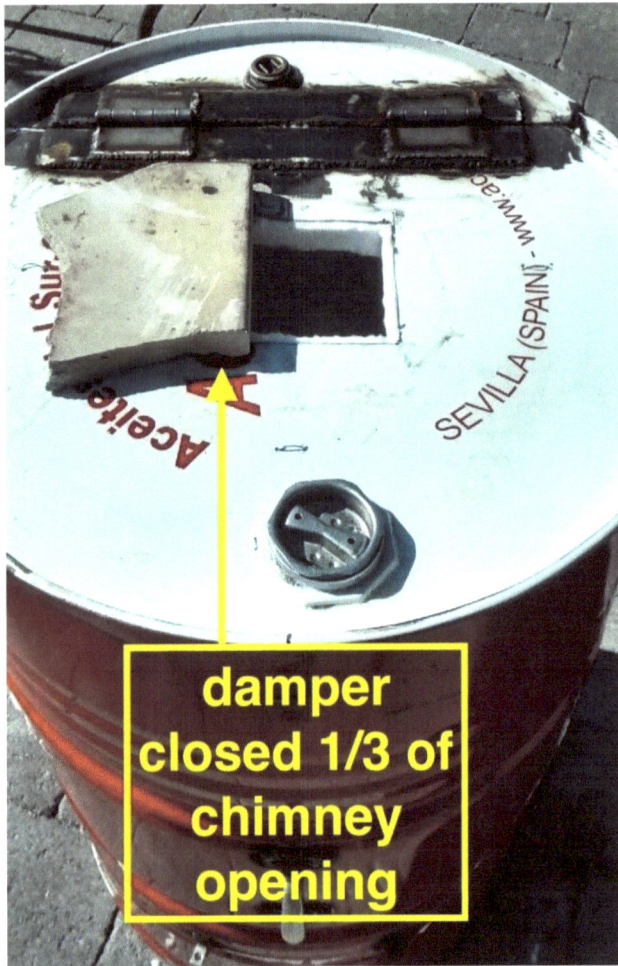
Figure 24: Damper for the chimney

Congratulations—you've built a Happy Barrel Raku Kiln!

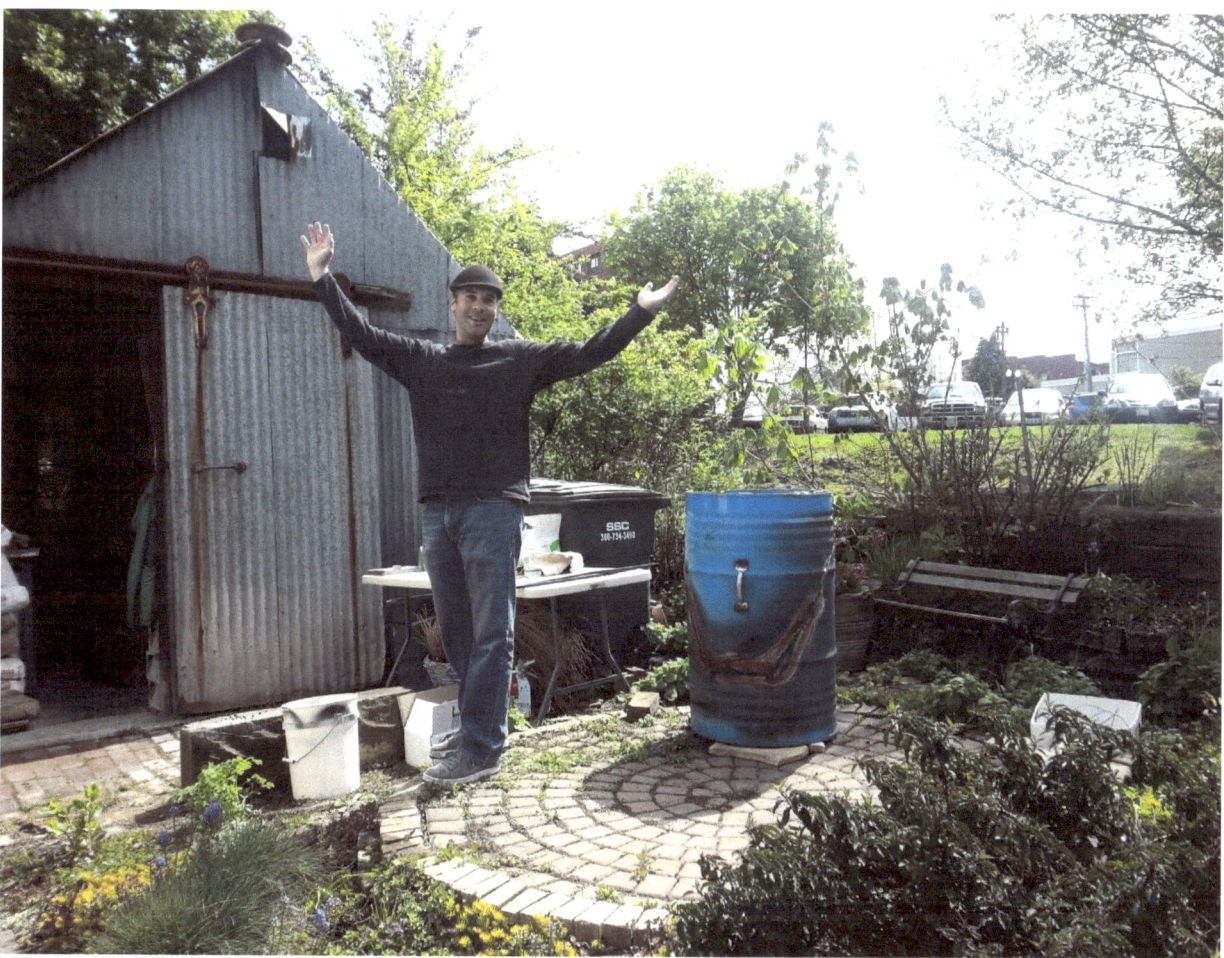

Burners

Burners come in all shapes and sizes, so depending on your budget you may choose a specific burner.

The cheapest and most readily available burner is a weed burner. These can be found at most hardware stores for very cheap. The efficiency of this kiln allows for this to be a great option on a budget.

For a more powerful burner, a venturi burner is a great option. This burner will be easier to get to the required temperature and will also give you the option of taking the kiln to higher temperatures depending on the rating of your fiber.

Maintenance and Care

Now that you've built your kiln, it's best to take care of it. It is best to feed your kiln on a regular basis to keep up with its appetite for raku firings!

Rain, snow, and the elements can damage your fiber over time, so it is best to make a cover for the top. This can be a metal garbage can lid, a piece of sheet metal, a barbeque fabric cover, or even just a large plastic bag (if the kiln is cool). Get creative!

Over time, the metal will lose its paint and start to rust. For the most part this isn't an issue, but if you are concerned about it you can use a heat resistant paint to coat the outside of the kiln. (Rust-Oleum has a fireplace paint and spray paint.)

Due to the thermal shock of raku firings and opening a kiln at those temperatures, your shelves, buttons, and bricks will have to be replaced. Depending on your clay and the shelves that you put in it, you might replace one or two buttons and a shelf every two years if you fire every week for two years.

Firing tips

Although this book is not intended as a firing manual, here are a few tips to get you started.

- SAFETY, SAFETY, SAFETY. Be in a safe spot for firing where nothing else will catch on fire. And keep water and a fire extinguisher handy just in case.

- ALWAYS, ALWAYS, ALWAYS make sure there is flame present and available when turning on the gas to your burner. Explosions can occur if the kiln is full of gas and is then lit.

- Your firing should take 45 minutes to an hour. Turn up the gas every 20 minutes or so and pay special attention to the sound of the burner.

- With a 20 pound propane tank, you should be able to get 2-3 firings. As the tank gets lower, it will begin to freeze. This is where it is important to listen to the roar of your burner when it is on full. When the tank freezes and the kiln starts to lose temperature, pour warm water slowly over the tank and you will hear the burner roar again.

- Top to bottom temperatures can be regulated with the damper. When it is cooler on top, close the damper slightly. Cooler on bottom, then open the damper slightly. Generally speaking, don't worry about top to bottom temperature until the kiln has reached around 1500° F.

About the Author

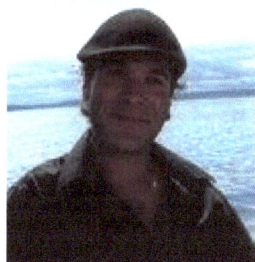

Originally from Wisconsin, Jesse grew up in a small community surrounded by the vast forests of the Kickapoo River valley.

Initially pursuing a career in aviation, Jesse discovered the world of art a few years into his time at Minnesota State University. In 2008, Jesse graduated from MSU with a Bachelor of Fine Arts, after which he moved to Australia to pursue a postgraduate degree in ceramics. His work continued to become a microcosmic representation of how he sees the world as a connected and interrelated source of creativity.

In 2011, Jesse returned to the United States and moved to Bellingham, WA, where he teaches ceramics and works as a professional artist.

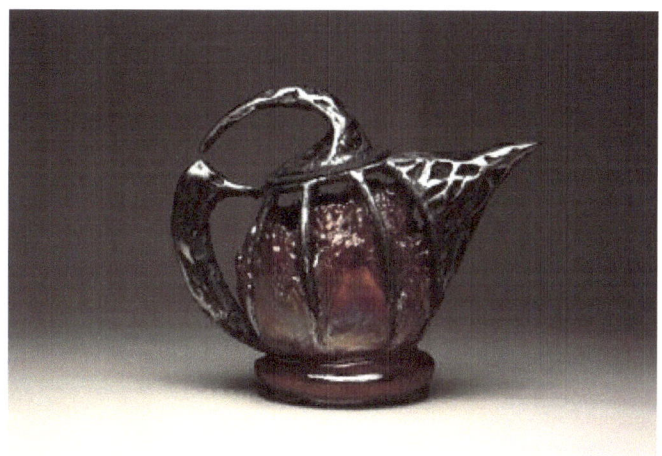
Figure 25: Wave Teapot. Raku fired Ceramics and Steel.

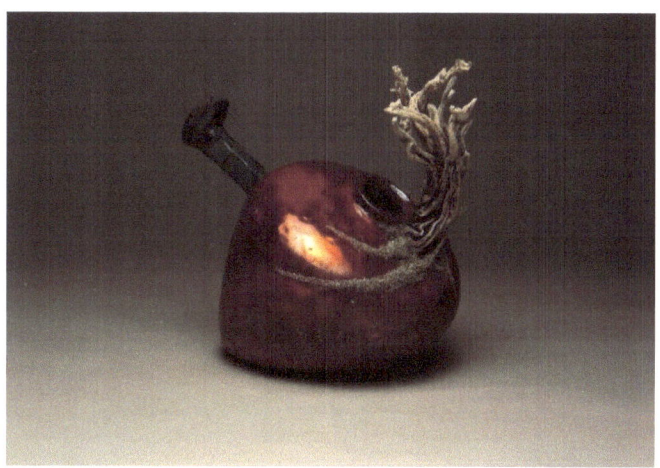
Figure 26: Old Growth Blood Mask. Raku fired Ceramics, Steel and found object.

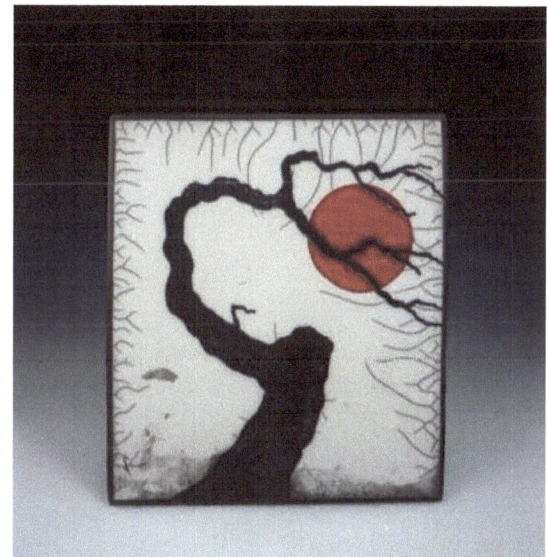
Figure 27: Wall hanging Tree Tile. Raku fired.

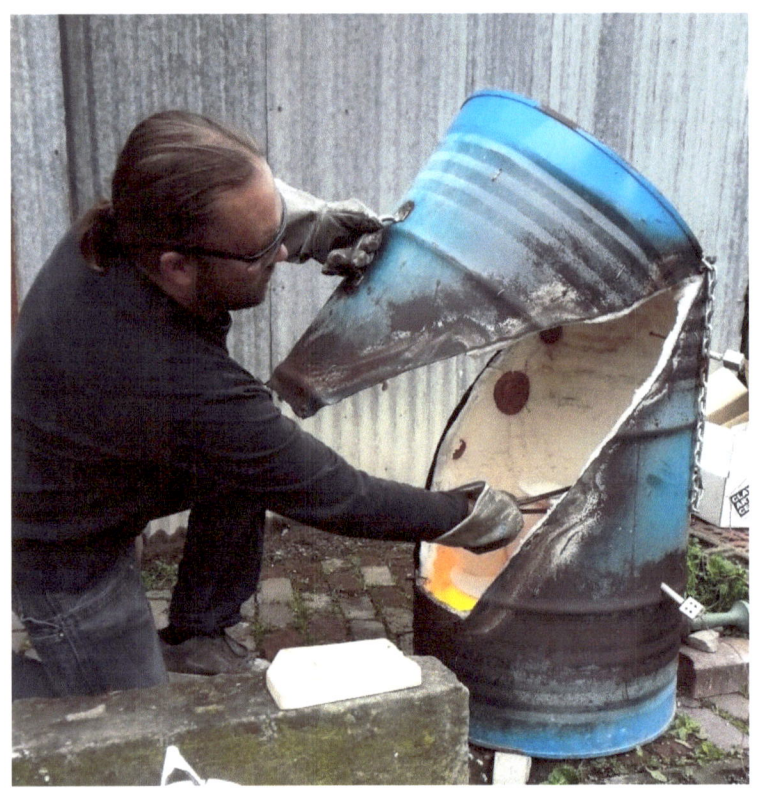
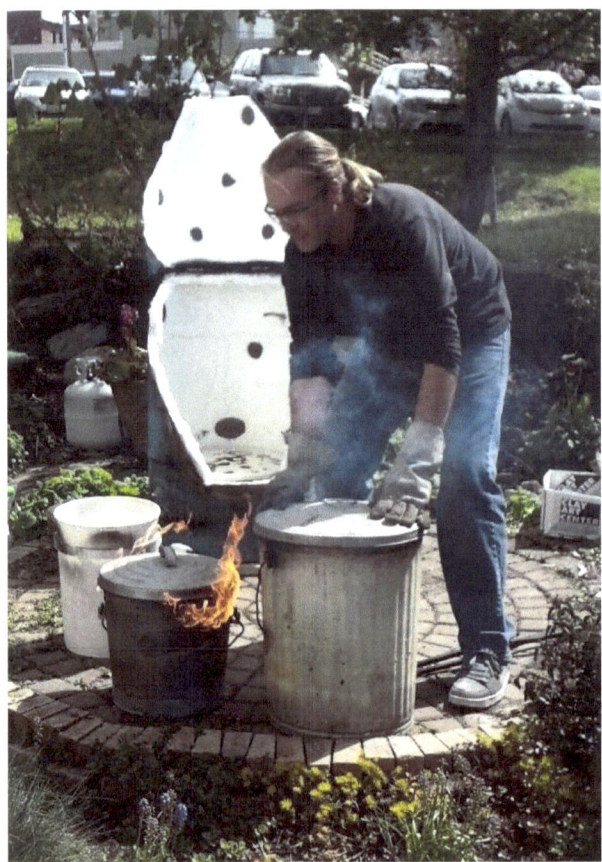

www.ingramcontent.com/pod-product-compliance
Lightning Source LLC
Chambersburg PA
CBHW051831210526
45473CB00005B/1822